MAKE TOMORROW BETTER

Joe Gorman

Visit Joe Gorman at his website: josephpatrickgorman.com
Visit his Author Page, Joe Gorman, on Facebook
Please add him on Twitter: @JoeJoegorman
Add him on Instagram at josephpatrickgorman
Please add a review on Amazon or Goodreads. Thanks!

ISBN: 1546645160
ISBN 13: 9781546645160

MEET PEOPLE WHERE THEY ARE

Meet people where they are. We can love someone, but we cannot make choices for them. Once we realize that we bear no responsibility for other people's choices and the consequences of those choices, we become less angry and more peaceful, less worried and more relaxed. We gain clarity and feel less confused. We realize that the energy we have spent attempting to change others can now be accessed to change ourselves in positive ways. The past is over and cannot be fixed by continuing to fret about it. Learn the lessons and grow into a healthier, happier person.

Make some time for yourself each day to develop your own identity, to access all your gifts, to become the full expression of your unique and beautiful being. Be yourself. Other people do not have to approve. *You* have to approve. If we remain discouraged from living our full being, we are sure to suffer boredom and depression. Our spirit will feel pressed down. You have unique gifts that only you can bring to our world. The only negative habits we should be concerned about are our own. Work on changing yourself. Be open minded and courageous, and face yourself. So much of our suffering is the result of holding on to resentments and other negative thinking. We can change that as soon as we wish.

All of us are on equal footing. Each of us has unique talents. No talent is of greater value than another. Do your part by offering your one-of-a-kind love, talent, and compassion to the wholeness of life.

STOP WISHING, START DOING

Our lives will become instantly better if we can find the inner strength to give up three bad habits:

1. Trying to control other people.
2. Seeking approval from others.
3. Our compulsion to judge others.

Once we understand that much of our pain and fear stems from these compulsions, we can move forward in life toward a deeper connection with ourselves and others. It may be a struggle at the beginning, but progress is rarely made without a struggle. Be humble enough to understand our limits, especially when it comes to attempting to change another person. If we turn inward and correct ourselves, the world changes. Happiness depends more on our dispositions than on outer circumstances.

Let go of everything you can't control. Practice being grateful for the many ways you are blessed. Relax. Is there any activity in your life that wouldn't become more enjoyable if you were relaxed? Find something in life that makes you happy to do every day. Promise yourself that you will be so strong that nothing will disturb your peace of mind. If you can't find peace and happiness inside yourself, you're not going to find it anywhere else. Stop wishing and start doing.

PROTECT YOURSELF FROM YOUR THOUGHTS

Protect yourself from your thoughts. We need to check ourselves frequently: is the turmoil we are feeling happening in real life, or is it happening only in our heads? We tend to construct elaborate inner fantasies in order to preserve the idea that we are kind. We play scenes from our past but with different outcomes. "I should have said this," or "I should have said that" are common fantasies. Realize that kind people can still say "No" frequently. Say it when the situation requires in real life rather than replaying the scenes over and over again in your thoughts. Speak your truth and be done with it. Other people may not like it, but you will feel healthier and happier.

If you are unhappy, something needs to change. Is the cause of your unhappiness circumstances in real life or thoughts that create anxiety and distress? One or the other must change. Move away from people and places that seem to be holding you down. You will soar to new heights once you remove people and places who are a drag on your life. Watch how people begin to value you more once you start to value yourself.

Believe that you can change your life. You can! Believe it, and you will no longer feel hopeless. When we change the way we look at things, the things we look at change. Make a firm commitment to become a more positive person. Life feels better when we retain a sense of optimism. Life feels better when we smile. Take better care of your spirit, and watch how your outer life improves.

YOU ARE RESPONSIBLE FOR YOUR OWN HAPPINESS

If you have someone in your life who isn't making you better, why are they still around? Why tolerate someone who discourages you, who weakens you by being offensive and relentlessly critical? When you realize exactly how valuable you are, you begin to sense how certain people bring you down. Find people who make you happy, who make life's burdens seem lighter, who encourage you to reach for new heights. Don't give up until you find them. If you're giving your all and it's not enough, you're probably giving it to the wrong person. Positivity is power. Negativity is an admission of weakness. Stay strong and hang only with people who lift you up.

Removing toxic people from our lives is an act of self-care. Certain people are so toxic to your spirit that there's nothing you can do except avoid them. Stop being who you were and become who you are. A positive first step is to shed anyone who is holding you back. Stop doing what isn't working. You are responsible for finding happiness.

Springtime and Easter are symbols of renewal. Trim away people, places, and things that are holding you down and be reborn. Be renewed. Become a more positive, loving, relaxed, and happy person. The path is right in front of you.

DEAL WITH YOUR OWN SET OF ISSUES

Have you heard the myth about a group of townspeople who was asked to pile all their woes and troubles in a big field behind the local high school? The town's mayor assured everyone that they could be permanently relieved of their own troubles as long as they were willing to exchange them for an equal number of their neighbors' troubles. Everyone was then given a chance to survey the mound of woes and eye up a number of troubles equal to what they had placed down. The citizens were happy to be able to dispense of their afflictions and looked forward to gathering up what they assumed would be a much lighter set of burdens placed down by their neighbors. They walked around and around the huge hill of problems, quietly surveying the issues of their friends and neighbors.

Finally, the mayor called for their attention. All he asked was that in a spirit of fairness, everyone should pick up a number of problems equal to what they had laid down. He gave them a signal to begin collecting from the pile of problems. Every single citizen quickly ran to regain his own woes and troubles. After seeing the issues that their friends and neighbors were dealing with, their own no longer seemed as much of a burden.

We have no idea what issues our friends and neighbors are quietly dealing with, and we shouldn't assume they have a lesser share than we do. Deal wisely with your own issues and work steadily to improve your life.

BE READY TO BE REBORN

Easter and springtime remind us that the natural cycle of life includes the death of our old selves, perhaps an extended period of dormancy, and then rebirth and renewal, sometimes in a completely different form. We see the phases of the moon, trees and flowers blooming, birds and bees and children growing. Why are we often so afraid of change? Are we worried that if life changes, we will no longer have our needs met? What is most puzzling is that we sometimes feel this way even when our needs are not being met currently. We still fear change. The basis of this fear is a lack of faith.

We owe it to ourselves to take the first steps toward our dreams. We don't have to see the entire staircase. We just have to find the courage to take one step at a time and to be firmly committed toward moving forward. We can make different choices today and trust that we will find the support we need to grow. Observe how nature is renewed. Trust. Have faith. We are here to help each other, comfort each other, offer sanctuary, and encourage each other to grow. Make a firm intention to grow and progress. Let life unfold toward peace and renewal. Smile, laugh, forgive, believe, and love. We don't have to be perfect, and we don't have to do anything perfectly. We have to trust that we are good enough. Like the trees and flowers, we will be made new as soon as we are brave enough to be reborn.

KEEP REACHING FOR YOUR HAPPINESS

Assume responsibility for your own happiness. Most of our afflictions come from our own thoughts. Our thoughts will torture us if we let them—so don't let them. Many perspectives on life float through our consciousness. Try giving your attention to only positive perspectives and see how quickly your outlook on life changes for the better. Are we deluding ourselves when we focus on the positive? No more than when we focus on thoughts that are relentlessly negative. We have one life. We will experience many joys and our measure of sorrows. It benefits us greatly to treat the inevitable highs and lows with a calm, peaceful, and encouraging attitude. Expect the best. If you are disappointed, learn the lesson and move forward.

Negative thoughts won't give you a positive life. Stop talking about your problems and start talking about your joys. Energy is contagious. Are you surrounded by people who encourage you to be your best? Do you spend time with people who reflect who you want to be and how you want to feel?

Stop focusing on your fears. You are going to be amazed at what you can accomplish once you start trusting yourself, encouraging yourself, and wholeheartedly believing in yourself. Handle the bad moments like the temporary setbacks they are. Maintain your poise and keep reaching for your happiness. Have faith, and take the first steps toward realizing your dreams.

A COWORKER'S HABITS ARE NOT YOUR PROBLEM

A coworker's work habits are not your problem, they're their problem—unless you allow yourself to be constantly annoyed by them and that becomes your problem. Your coworker isn't your problem, your desire to control others is your problem. You are volunteering for aggravation. Other people's problems are other people's problems. We aren't in control of them in even the slightest way unless we have been given explicit supervisory obligations to fix them. Has anyone at your company asked you specifically to modify a coworker's behavior? Has someone else been assigned to supervise them?

Live and let live. Spend your precious energy figuring out what you can do to be a more integral, essential worker. Spend your mental energy becoming a positive force for your business or workplace. Improve your own attitude and productivity. Don't be dragged down by anyone else.

Life will present us with plenty of challenges. Look for the joys in life, not challenges for which you have no responsibility or control over. The only mistakes that should concern us are our own. Every mistake contains a lesson for us. Instead of stressing out about it, absorb the lesson and move forward more wisely. Have you ever noticed yourself repeating a mistake when you should have known better? Maybe you were focusing too much attention on the mistakes of others rather than remaining conscious of your own. Zero in on what's in front of you today. Trying to improve yourself isn't selfish, it's smart. You are the only person in the world whom you can improve.

IS IT TIME TO MOVE ON?

I often hear people say, "I wish I were treated better." And the tendency is to look around and blame the people in their lives for not treating them better. But the solution remains inside us. Why are we hanging around people who do not treat us respectfully? How did we get to this place? Is our self-esteem so low that we've become comfortable around people who routinely criticize us and denigrate us, who ridicule us and put us down? Fortunately, a solution is always at hand.

Our first step is to look inside ourselves and realize that we deserve to be treated at all times with respect and honor. We need to quiet our mind and deeply realize and understand that moving forward means associating only with people who lift us up, who treat us with kindness and understanding.

Once we realize that our soul needs respect and kindness to feel at peace, the next step is to examine our close relationships and make sure we surround ourselves only with people who reflect who we want to be and how we want to feel. Energy is contagious, and people with toxic, negative energy have a way of making other people feel bad. Why spend one more moment with a person like this? Move on.

Once you remove a few people from your circle, you will feel lighter and happier. It won't be a coincidence. It may seem challenging to remove a few friends, but it is actually easier than remaining in a hurtful, negative cycle. Spend your energy on people and situations that move your life forward.

WE DESERVE LOVE

We deserve love. We deserve peace of mind. We deserve respect. When we are grounded, we can acknowledge these truths. Why is it that sometimes we believe we don't deserve them? Where does that negativity come from? It is difficult to fight an enemy who seems to reside in our head. Often, these doubts were planted by the very wounded adults who helped raise us, teach us, or coach us when we were too young and inexperienced to realize that adults aren't always right and are sometimes mean-spirited and cruel. So how do we move forward successfully in life? How do we shed these doubts that were planted when we were young and defenseless?

Realize that we are not in the world to live up to anybody else's expectations. Refuse to sacrifice who you are in order to make someone else happy. Your feelings matter and should be trusted more than anyone else's opinion. Trust yourself first and foremost. Speak your truth and honor your feelings. You are not being unreasonable when you insist on having your needs met. Your thoughts matter. Your insights matter. *You matter.* Remain unmoved by both praise and blame. How you feel about yourself is most important. Become sensitive to that, and you are on your way to being the strong, independent, uniquely gifted person you were born to become.

YOU HAVE TO FIND YOUR SOUL BEFORE YOU FIND YOUR SOULMATE

You have to find your soul before you find your soulmate. The chief impediment to finding our soul is our thoughts. The constant thought-chatter in our head paralyzes us. The moment our life becomes quiet, the thought squirrels start scampering. Often our thoughts remind us of our fears, of worst case scenarios, of reasons why we should be seeking revenge, of our disappointments in ourselves and others, of real or imagined losses. Thoughts magnify our obligations and make us feel overwhelmed. Thoughts often lead us to jump to a wrong conclusion. Much of our problem drinking and drug-seeking behaviors are desperate attempts to quiet our thoughts. What healthy habits can we practice to quiet our thoughts and find peace of mind?

A positive first step is realizing that our thoughts aren't true. Thoughts are not facts. They frequently are negative messages from disembodied voices from our past—leftover untruths from negative, toxic people we have moved away from. Pay no attention to them. Let these negative thoughts crumble. They aren't real. Choose thoughts that empower you to become a stronger, more loving, more peaceful person. Focus on thoughts that serve you. Do not serve your thoughts.

Your soul is in command of your life; your thinking is not. Meditation, prayer, yoga, readings from spiritual texts, a positive mantra, breathing exercises, and a firm commitment to positivity can all help us manage our thoughts and find peace. When our minds become peaceful, our lives become peaceful. When our lives are directed by our souls, we become kinder, happier, and more relaxed.

ARE YOU SURROUNDED BY PEOPLE WHO MAKE YOU FEEL GOOD?

Nothing can dim the light that shines within us. But that doesn't mean people won't try. Today let's give some thought to the people in our lives and the effects each person has on our mood. Some people never fail to lift our spirits. Energy is contagious, and when we see loved ones we feel our spirits soar. Just the thought of certain people will bring a smile to our face. But there are certain other people who have the opposite effect. Seeing them tends to bring us down. They are a drag to our spirits and mood.

Take an inventory of your circle of friends. It might be time to tighten your circle. Looking back on our lives, we see that we outgrew certain people. We no longer had enough mutual interests, or maybe our dreams just took us in another direction. That's all right. We are not here to please others and they're not here to please us. But we'd be foolish to continue hanging with people or in places that drag our spirit down. Disconnect from negative people and watch how your life improves. You will feel better and achieve more once you shed the weight of negativity. Life is too short to stress over people who don't deserve to be part of your life. A positive life is a process. Part of that process is moving away from people who dull our shine. Are you surrounded by people who make you feel good?

You don't have to be who anybody else wants you to be. You are free to be whomever you want to be. Move forward with your encouragers, and ditch the toxic discouragers.

DO WE WANT TO BE BITTER OR BETTER?

A quick glance at the natural world shows that everything in life has many chances to be reborn and transformed. If we are willing to search inside ourselves and work on changing the only person in the world we have any chance of changing—ourselves—we can become less anxious and worried because we realize that all change comes from a willingness to be transformed.

Each of us has a unique mission. Once we become courageous enough to accept that we are in charge of only ourselves, we can allow our worried, insecure, confused, angry, and resentful parts to pass away, and we become reborn as a lighter, more confident person.

Do we want to be bitter or better? When we stop trying to move the mountain, our relationship with the mountain changes. Inner peace comes from realizing there are parts of life we cannot change (other people's decisions and behaviors) and parts of life we can change (our own decisions and behaviors). We can't fix other people. We can take full responsibility for our own lives and change direction any time we choose.

If our love and compassion do not include ourselves, they are incomplete. Inner peace and true happiness come only from within. We can't remake the world, but we have all the power necessary to remake ourselves. Let's work on fixing ourselves, with a spirit of compassion and love.

AN ATTITUDE OF GRATITUDE

It's a mistake to think that when we are unhappy or uneasy, we must not have enough of something. Focusing on what we think we lack is a sure way to remain unhappy. Focusing on the many reasons we all have to be grateful is the path to happiness. Being satisfied with our current blessings makes us feel good. Why, then, does our mind seem to return to a sense of lack when we feel unsettled?

When we are hungry, angry, lonely, or tired, our sense of lack often becomes acute. Advertisers exploit this by trying to convince us that we will become happier if we drive a new car, take a cruise, eat at a certain restaurant chain, or own the latest gadget. Studies show that we will indeed feel happier for a short while after a large purchase, but then our mood will flat line and we will be left right where we are, facing our unsettled feelings and now faced with paying off the debt we incurred from the new purchase. How long will it take to pay off those ten days of happiness?

A hug from a child, a kiss from a loved one, good health, an appreciation for nature, and the conscious practice of gratitude will all provide happiness that will not fade. And they're free! Count your blessings, not your problems. Appreciate what you do have instead of longing for what you don't have. An attitude of gratitude always leads to happiness.

LIFE GOES BY TOO QUICKLY TO WASTE TIME ON NEGATIVE THINKING

Life goes by too quickly to waste time on negative thinking. Try to go 24 hours without complaining. You'll be amazed at how your life starts changing. You'll feel better, too. Allowing negativity into your life is usually a choice. Don't feel guilty about distancing yourself from people who hurt you. Do what helps you to grow.

Today you find yourself where your thoughts have brought you. Where will your thoughts take you tomorrow? Believe in yourself. There is one corner of the world that we can be certain of improving, and that's our own corner. Change in life is unavoidable, so create the change that you wish to see in your own life. Be strong enough and grounded enough that another person cannot possibly bring you down. The Constitution gives us the right to pursue happiness, but you have to catch it yourself.

Fate may determine who enters your life, but you determine who stays. Cherish the people who cherish you. If someone rejects you, it says nothing about you and everything about them and their insecurities and limitations. They weren't blessed with the strength to handle you. Move forward toward happiness.

NOBODY'S PERFECT

An essential step in becoming a grounded and mature human being is accepting that we have never been perfect. Our mistakes were learning experiences, and we have grown wiser and stronger because of them. We need to practice humility and realize we can never be perfect. But despite our stumbles and weaknesses, we continue to grow. Accepting our own imperfection allows us to become more tolerant of the blind spots and weaknesses of others. Setting impossible and unrealistic goals for ourselves or others is certain to bring us frustration and unhappiness. If we intend to be happy, let's first admit that we are never going to be perfect.

We all have regrets. Our imperfect nature and ego has led us to leave jobs and friends that we may miss very much. Perhaps we missed an opportunity to help a friend or coworker when he or she needed us. We may have passed on good opportunities because of laziness or a negative attitude. Dwelling on past mistakes is usually fruitless. Learn the lesson and move forward. The past cannot be changed. Start responding to today's challenges with an open mind and a positive attitude. Make a promise to yourself that you will become more conscious today. Become an instrument of peace and positivity in your family, your workplace, and your relationships.

GIVE PEACE A CHANCE

Give peace a chance. Have you ever made a firm commitment to yourself to remain peaceful? Life is experienced better that way. We are responsible for our own feelings. If we get too deeply involved in another person's feelings, we can lose track of our own. When someone we love is angry and ranting, we often feel a storm starting to brew in our own feelings. When we have porous boundaries, we are sometimes overwhelmed by the anger and confusion of a loved one. If we are not cautious and conscious, we can lose touch with our own feelings and become swept up in their fear, despair, or anger. When we have porous boundaries, we become less capable of offering the calm support our loved ones need. Other people are entitled to their feelings, but we are entitled to maintain an emotional equilibrium.

People may say they "have a right to be upset." But we have a right to remain peaceful. We don't have to share anyone's resentment. Once we start sharing the resentment of others, we lose track of our own peace and happiness. Don't allow other people to manipulate your emotional state. Resentment is self-harming and self-defeating. If we are determined to maintain our own inner peace and happiness, we can observe others' emotional distress without permitting it to cause any of our own.

FOCUS ON THE POSITIVE

Don't let your mind focus on the next thing you dread. Don't ruin the present by catastrophizing the future. Anxiety is present whenever we find the courage to attempt something new. It is natural and normal to be anxious about buying a house, going away to college, starting a new school, putting our signature on a car loan, or joining the armed forces. Many people experience anxiety when they are engaging in circumstances beyond their personal control, such as flying in an airplane or riding a roller coaster. Anything exciting carries with it a grain of anxiety.

But anxiety should not paralyze us. We know from past experiences that many tasks that once seemed impossible or intimidating (driving a car for the first time, learning a new language, learning how to swim) were eventually mastered and have rewarded us with their utility and convenience. Anxiety that paralyzes us has its roots in our thinking. Our thoughts will ruin our days if we let them. Choose only thoughts that are encouraging and positive.

We can reorient our lives toward optimism and hope. Let negative thoughts dissolve and replace them with positive, life-affirming thoughts. Relax and believe. Don't rush. Rushing creates doubt. Your life will change when you change your thinking. Take an inventory of all your talents and skills. See, you are capable of learning and doing and achieving great things that bring you great pleasure. Doubt your doubts, not your faith. Whatever we plant in our minds and make a sincere commitment to mastering will come to pass. Our intentions become our reality. The first step in getting somewhere is deciding that you're not going to stay where you are. We evolve through our struggles. Embrace the challenge and keep your thoughts only on the positive. You can do this.

PLAN PLANS, NOT RESULTS

Plan plans, not results. We can try our best in every situation. We can wake up each day and make a firm intention to be a better spouse, parent, friend, or coworker. Instead of going out of our way to criticize people, we can go out of our way to support them. We can refuse to allow negativity in our life and vow to be an instrument of peace and positivity. But we cannot save another person from his or her own destructive habits. We can love someone with our entire heart and soul but accept the fact that we cannot save anyone but ourselves. Sometimes that means detaching with love rather than enabling someone to use us to continue their self-destructive slide into oblivion. All the king's horses and all the king's men cannot stop someone from engaging in self-destructive habits through their own free will.

When someone passes away or gets into serious trouble, there is a tendency to think, "I should have done more," or "I should have been there for them," even though we have loved them to the best of our patience and capabilities. We planned to love them and we did love them. In the past, we may have been naive enough to help enable their self-destructive habits. But we cannot blame ourselves if our love was not enough to stop their own free will from continuing to make self-harming choices. We cannot make choices for anyone but ourselves. Our loved ones can make their own choices and then experience the consequences of those choices. If the consequence of their self-harming behavior is death or a loss of freedom, we can grieve, mourn, pray, and love, but it's self-harming on our part to engage in the fantasy that we could have stopped them.

WE ARE IN CHARGE OF ONLY OURSELVES

We can't control the hearts and minds of others—an indelible truth that many of us struggle to accept. Why doesn't this certain person like me? I am so good for them. Why won't someone I love stop using drugs or alcohol? Shouldn't my love be enough to stop them? Sadly, we aren't in charge of anyone's heart or mind except our own. When we realize this absolute truth, we begin moving toward experiencing peace in our own mind and heart.

Have you ever made a strong promise to yourself to go on a diet? To start going to the gym five times a week? To start jogging? We set these goals with the very best of intentions to improve ourselves. Weeks pass and we take an inventory. Are we following our new diet every day? Going to the gym? Jogging? Our best laid plans for ourselves are often in shambles just a few months later. We can acknowledge, hopefully with a sense of humor, that change is very hard.

It's an enormous challenge to change ourselves. It's an impossible dream to change anyone else. If we can barely summon the strength and willpower to change ourselves, let's agree that it is absolutely futile to attempt to change anyone else. We are in charge of only our own hearts and minds. It's all we can do to quiet our mind enough to realize how we truly feel about a person or situation. We will never be able to impact how someone else feels. Choose a path of peace. Take care of your own heart and mind and let everyone else take care of theirs.

RELIEVING STRESSFUL FEELINGS IS POSSIBLE

Relieving stressful feelings is possible. It starts with a firm commitment to having peaceful thoughts. Or are you committed to panic? Sometimes we made adaptations to cope with certain unavoidable stresses when we were younger and now we unconsciously maintain those coping strategies even though they no longer serve us. If nothing changes, then nothing changes. What will you have to change in order to feel more at ease? Do you consciously begin each day with a commitment to being an instrument of peace in our world? Peace begins with being patient with ourselves. Do you extend the same love and patience to yourself as you do to significant others? If your compassion and love do not include you, they're incomplete.

Inner peace begins with forgiving others, including ourselves. Are your thoughts healing? Let go of any fear or resentment. Don't cling to negative experiences. Understand the brevity of life—your own and everybody else's—and act accordingly. Realize that your happiness depends on you. Practice feeling peaceful and positive about life. Gain a sense of how connected we all are, but don't worry if others are not as enthused about life as you are. We will never completely calm our mind, but we can stop identifying with its agitations. Practice peace.

IMAGINE

Imagine how much more peaceful our lives would be if we just minded our own business. Imagine if we all used our energy to make positive changes to our own life rather than prescribe changes we think others should make to their lives. Letting other people, including family members, be who they are will free a big stream of energy so we can make positive changes in our own life. What if we stopped worrying about the speck of sawdust in our brother's eye and started doing something about the log in our own eye that blinds us to our own imperfections and self-defeating behaviors? We will be free to be who we are and allow others the freedom to be who they are.

A positive life is a process, not a state of being. It is a direction that we walk toward, not a destination where we become static and complacent. Each of us has potential that no one else has. And it is not enough to wish for change. Change is an action that requires intention, focus, and energy. Become energized. Make a commitment to see the positive changes you dream about by exerting the energy and making a sincere commitment to bring these changes to reality. Live the life you've imagined. This might be good time to shed the negative people and habits that are holding you back. Tighten your circle and eliminate anyone who is not a positive, encouraging influence. You do not have to be who anyone else wants you to be. You are free to be you. Please grant others the freedom to be who they are. The world will become a more positive and peaceful place.

INNER PEACE

Inner peace begins when we decide not to allow another person or event to disturb our emotions. We are in charge of our life. When we wake up to face our day, we can take a quick inventory of what we hope to accomplish in the next sixteen hours. If we believe in a Higher Power, we can ask for guidance and strength. We can ask to become a channel of God's peace. We can make a personal commitment not to add to the confusion of the world, but rather to be a force that brings clarity and insight to others. We can realize that we will face plenty of challenges and adventures today that need our undivided energy and attention. We do not have to worry about what tomorrow or next week will bring. Today is a challenging enough portion of life to tackle. Tomorrow's challenges will all still be waiting for us tomorrow.

We have sixteen hours to be a force of positive energy and love. We do not have to solve anyone else's challenges—just our own. If someone we care about is in a negative frame of mind or a dark mood, it is not up to us to draw them out of it or respond to their challenges. We are given plenty of energy each day to respond to our own challenges. We will feel depleted and exhausted if we respond to other people's challenges as well. Let's deal with our own issues and allow everyone else the opportunity for personal growth while dealing with their own issues. Stay focused on your own life, your own challenges, your own emotions, your own intentions. You will be amazed at how much positive energy, optimism about life, and laser-like focus we can access when we take care of our own business each day.

TAKE CONTROL OF YOUR LIFE

We can't change the past but we can upset a perfectly fine present by worrying about the future. Worry has never influenced any event for the better. Worry saps our power and strength. It distracts us from what we should be focusing on to ensure our success. Problems are not the problem. Finding a courageous, positive way to handle each problem is a daily challenge. It is a challenge that we are given every possible tool, trait, and skill to meet. Stop focusing on the problem and start focusing on a positive resolution to your troubles.

The only person coming to save you is you. You will grow and gain wisdom by facing each problem honestly and directly. Accept what challenges come and meet them with your best brave effort. Direct your energy and attention toward change and stop fretting. No matter what we've done or where we've been, every single one of us can change by making a firm intention to change. Take control of your life. Create the future you've dreamed about. Will your future be problem free? Most definitely not. But you will understand that you have all the power, courage, and focus necessary to overcome whatever life puts in your way. What we focus on expands. Focus on what helps you grow. Replace any negative thought with a positive one, and watch how your life changes for the better.

DO THE NEXT RIGHT THING

Sometimes a goal seems so far away that we become disheartened and discouraged to the point of telling ourselves it is futile to pursue it for even one more minute. But that is a self-defeating behavior. We can always do the next right thing that will bring us an inch, an hour, or an ounce closer to achieving a dream. Realizing a dream is rarely easy. We have to expect tough challenges, brief setbacks, and hours when we must summon every ounce of courage, patience, and determination available.

When we are attempting something exceptionally challenging, we may not hear the encouragement we need from others. Remember that it's your dream, not theirs. This journey is yours alone. The first step in gaining the faith of others is having a strong faith in yourself. This path is meant for your feet alone. We can't blame others for not seeing the path to our dream as clearly as we can. Do the next right thing. If you are feeling frustrated waiting for a partner or associate to complete a task you've hired them to do or if their time line isn't perfectly synced with your time line, do some research that will broaden your understanding of your new venture. You will be entering new territory, so get a head start on learning the lay of the land while your partner completes their task. Prepare for the next step you're going to take after your partner completes their appointed assignment.

Abraham Lincoln said, "Give me six hours to chop down a tree and I will spend the first four hours sharpening the axe." Sharpen your axe. Get ready. If we take a few steps each day, in due time our dream will come true. Do the next right thing right now.

BECOME ALL THAT YOU CAN BECOME

When you encounter a problem, trust your competence. Don't settle for what's comfortable. Take a risk and go for what you always wanted. And don't be too hard on yourself. There are plenty of people willing to do that for you. It's critical that we disconnect from other people's negative energy. No matter what happens, no matter how far away you seem to be from your goal, don't stop believing that you will somehow make it. Most of the stuff we worry about never happens. Every time we awaken, we are presented with another day to do things right.

Believe that the best is yet to come. Relax, let the universe present the time and the way, and watch how quickly you start to make progress. What holds most people back isn't the quality of their ideas, it's their lack of faith in their own competence. If we don't strongly believe in ourselves, how can we expect others to believe in our ideas? Lead the way. Have faith in yourself. Confidence is a magnet that will attract the supporters you need. You have a singular gift, and the life experiences that only you have lived have prepared you to share this gift with others. Use those unique experiences to fulfill your great potential. Be prepared to be all that you can be.

SHOW UP FOR YOUR OWN LIFE

Show up for your own life. Accept your current circumstances. The first step in moving beyond our current predicament is fully and truthfully admitting where we are. We have to accept reality before we can change it. Now we ask: what do we intend to change? How important is this change? If we say it's important, then it should be written down and referred to a few times each day so that we retain our focus.

Change creates anxiety. And anxiety is so unpleasant that we welcome any distraction from it. Growth is scary. Taking the next step forward is scary. Part of our unconscious mind will welcome being distracted from our anxiety, but remember that we are really being distracted from change and growth—two essentials we intend to pursue. Writing down our circumstance-altering goal is a positive reminder that we are mature enough and ready to move forward. A strong goal is to make two changes each day that move us forward, away from our current (unpleasant) circumstances so we are changing in the present. Where are we headed in the future? Where would you like to be a month from now? A year from now? Five years from now?

Develop a strong mental image and set a firm intention. Keep your eyes on the prize. Write down your long-term goals also. At the end of each day, find a quiet minute and review your day's progress. Did you gain ground? Did you move forward toward a better future? Our minds will assist us even while we sleep if we keep a firm intention to grow into change.

WE ARE NOT HERE TO LIVE UP TO ANYONE'S EXPECTATIONS

Focus on what disturbs you and you'll always be disturbed. No one is here to live up to our expectations—not our spouse or significant other, not our children, not the guys who pick up our trash. We are setting ourselves up for wave after wave of disappointment if we refuse to acknowledge that we are not in charge of anyone's life but our own. If you want other people to do exactly as you wish, you'll have to direct a film. In real life, we are actors living among billions of other actors. When other people's actions displease us, it is self-harming to take it personally.

Everyone stumbles because each of us has character defects. We start the day hoping to hit the mark, but we often fall short of our own expectations. It is futile to expect someone else to live up to our expectations. If we allow our minds to be agitated by the character defects of others, our days and nights will remain agitated. The only character defects we are in charge of eliminating are our own. It is tempting to distract ourselves from our own failings by staying focused on the failings of others.

Our lives will improve significantly when our thinking improves significantly. We can't change what we refuse to acknowledge. Our happiness depends on improving our own thinking and actions, not improving the thinking and actions of anyone else. When we learn patience, gratitude, self-confidence, and optimism, we become happier. When we keep our sense of humor, we become happier. When we stay focused on the present, we become happier. Try it and you'll see.

MAKING AMENDS

We can't change the past—neither ours nor anyone else's. If we have past behaviors that haunt us, we have to find a way to discharge that energy and move forward. Everyone has committed actions that were unskilled and hurtful to others. Sometimes we can make amends to the people we hurt, but sometimes we have to be mature enough to realize that any attempt to make amends will reopen old wounds and stir up more trouble. So, what can we do?

A first step is to find a way to forgive ourselves. We can't change what we did. We can reflect on our past actions and gain new insights into our current behavior. We can be cautious not to fall into the trap of the unconscious thinking and blind reactions that led us to commit the unskilled behavior. We can accept what we did and reflect on making changes to ourselves that will ensure that we don't commit the same mistake again.

It is always beneficial to become more conscious of our behaviors and attitudes. The more conscious we become, the better our life will flow in positive directions. If we reflect on our past behaviors and motives and learn to forgive ourselves for our blindness, we will regain good, positive energy that has been clamped off and frozen.

We can't change the past, but we can make amends by using the new energy to make a more positive contribution to our current life. Yesterday can't be changed. Today can. We can volunteer to lend our talents to others. We can help our neighbors. We can clean up debris and litter in our community. We can beautify our property. We can visit the sick. We can write a letter to someone who is in prison. We can use our energies to add to the world's goodness and balance out a time when we acted selfish and unskilled.

YOU CAN'T FIX ME AND I CAN'T FIX YOU

You can't fix me and I can't fix you. I can fix me and you can fix you by following positive living principles that are tried and true. What are some of these principles that will make our lives and our outlook better?

Keep your mind and focused—not on your disappointments, but on people, places, and experiences that you love. Hang with people who have the same positive energy and goal-directed outlook as you. Don't let negative thinking detract from your happiness. Always stay positive and always move forward. Walk away from drama and keep your circle positive. Realize that your value will never be determined by other people. Visualize success and find out what steps you need to take to arrive there. Decide what you want to give instead of what you want to get. Realize that the less you respond to negative people, the more peaceful your day will be. Surround yourself with people who encourage you to be your best. Pull away from negative, toxic people and see how quickly your outlook on life changes. Let only people you completely trust into your inner circle. Not everyone deserves a seat at your table.

Realize that your future is wide open and undecided. If you can dream it, you can be it. Your success depends on you, so take smart, positive, helpful steps each day toward reaching it. Perhaps you can't realize your dream today, but you can most definitely take a few steps toward moving closer to its realization.

Relax and breathe. You're going to get there soon.

DEEPEN YOUR APPRECIATION

If we always do what we've always done, we'll always get what we always got. How much of our life is driven by sometimes subtle and sometimes desperate activities that are attempts to lessen our anxiety? Drinking. Drugging. Running from here to there. Hanging out with people we're not even sure we like. Buying this, buying that. An endless stream of diversions—video games, television series, YouTube videos, and social media posts.

Why do we put so much effort into fleeing from our feelings? The uncomfortable feelings remain, and we awaken realizing that we've spent too much money again, took risks that we immediately regretted, or spent another evening with people who use us, abuse us, and can't be trusted to ever put our needs first. Why? We spent another night of our lives having fun but realizing at our core that we felt unfulfilled and unhappy even in the midst of all the clamor. How do we step out of this ceaseless, unsatisfying search for relief, peace, and happiness?

The first step is the most challenging: to realize that we have to find ways to be at peace. No one can provide peace for us. Frantic, manic activities are distractions, not true peace. Our initial uneasy feelings are still here and often are amplified by new feelings of guilt, disappointment, and rejection.

Seek peace. Find a way to quiet your thoughts. Meditate. It's not that difficult to stay quiet for fifteen minutes. Breathe deeply. Set up a small shrine or altar. Connect with your own spirit and the spirits of loved ones who truly will protect you and care for you. Love yourself. We are all imperfect. Nourish your spirit. Our feelings are fountains of wisdom. Get to know yourself and deepen your love and appreciation for who you truly are.

Made in the USA
San Bernardino, CA
29 June 2017